On the Watch

...Praying for the imminent revival

All rights reserved. No part of this publication may be reproduced, stored in a retrieval system or transmitted, in any form or by any means without the prior permission in writing of the author or as expressly permitted by law, or under terms agreed with the appropriate reprographics rights organisation.

Enquiries concerning reproduction outside the scope of the above should be sent to the author. You must not circulate this book in any other binding or cover, and you must impose this same condition on any acquirer.

Produced by Bytels Publishing
Printed in the United Kingdom
Copyright © 2018 Bunmi Adekeye

Scripture quotations marked NIV are taken from the Holy Bible, New International Version®, NIV® Copyright © 1973, 1978, 1984, 2011 by Biblica, Inc.®. Used by permission of Zondervan. All rights reserved worldwide.

Scripture quotations marked (NLT) are taken from the Holy Bible, New Living Translation, copyright © 1996, 2004, 2007, 2013, 2015 by Tyndale House Foundation. Used by permission of Tyndale House Publishers, Inc., Carol Stream, Illinois 60188. All rights reserved.

Scripture quotations marked NKJV are taken from the New King James Version®. Copyright © 1982 by Thomas Nelson. Used by permission. All rights reserved.

DEDICATION

To the One who called me out of darkness into His marvellous light; the King of all kings and Lord of all lords, the One to whom I owe everything, my creator and redeemer, the One who inspired me to write this book.

To my late parents who took me to church from a very tender age and whose values gave me the initial exposure to Christianity, a factor which eventually led me to seek God.

To my wonderful husband and co-labourer, my greatest fan and cheerleader who always stands by me and encourages me to press on with whatever the Lord has placed upon my heart.

To the leaders and members of City Gates Church, Ilford who for the past 17 years have supported me in my journey with the Lord and without whom you would not be reading this book.

To the Church universal whom I long to see united as Christ prayed for us; walking in His fullness; and influential as salt and light again in this world.

ACKNOWLEDGEMENTS

I would like to appreciate:

Velveta and Steve Thompson for allowing me to share a bit of their story. I could never tell it like they would but then I cannot do justice to the account of this journey without sharing how it all started. In those dark days, Steve stood strong; not only did he encourage us by telling us what to pray about, he gave us insight into the power of praise as a battle weapon.

Bola Abiloye who rolled up her sleeves and stepped up as co-administrator as soon as I shared the idea of praying for Velveta with her. Partnering with her has been a joy and I honestly do not know how we would have got to where we are today without her, especially in those early days when multiple things were moving simultaneously at a fast pace. With minimal prior experience, we both had to rapidly learn as we went along how to maintain some order within a large group whilst allowing the free flow of the Holy Spirit.

The City Gates Church members who heard and responded to the clarion call to pray for Velveta when the doctors offered no hope and all we could cling to was the unfailing word of God. These faithful children of God were relentless and continued to press on for many more weeks after our original prayer had been answered.

Pastor Gareth Sherwood who managed the communications in the darkest hour; he was able to maintain a balance between giving us enough information to help us know how to pray without the gruesome details which could cause our faith to waver. He was the one who broke to me the best news of answered prayer I had ever heard and he has not let me forget how dramatic my reaction was.

Pastor Steve Derbyshire, our Lead Pastor at City Gates Church who recognises the gifting in his congregation members and facilitates growth by encouraging us to step out into what the Lord has called us to. Without any hesitation he gave us his blessing and full endorsement to continue this prayer ministry once the idea was presented to him.

The brothers and sisters on the watchtower who chose to remain in the place of constant unending prayer for our nation after we had received the healing we had been praying for; the faithfulness of these sons and daughters of God constantly challenges me to keep pressing on.

Kayode, my husband who believes in me and supports

all my ventures, he was the first to go through this book, painstakingly editing it and giving me his feedback.

My sister, Pastor Ronke Olulana, who suggested that I should write a two-page document about this journey; little did I know that my short document would balloon into a short book.

Sackey Bennin, the eagle-eyed member of the watchtower prayer group who thoroughly went through the manuscript for this book, editing it for language, consistency and flow.

Without the Lord stirring up the hearts of all the afore-mentioned people and steering us in the path He has ordained for us, we would not have the awesome experiences that brought about this book. To Him be all the glory, honour and praise forever and ever.

FOREWORD

It was said of the early church that they *devoted themselves to prayer*. There was no need for leaders to encourage or initiate this prayer movement because it was inspired by the Holy Spirit. Through the power of the Holy Spirit these first century believers were convinced they could change nations through prayer.

During the summer of 2017 something very significant happened in City Gates Church. What began in response to an individual's need for healing became a prayer initiative to see our nation changed by the power of God and continues to this day.

I have the privilege of leading City Gates Church and have been amazed how the watchtower has resonated in the hearts of many, from tentative small beginnings to what it has now become. Whether you are a leader or church member, I hope you will be inspired by Bunmi's story. These are days for believing like John Wesley, that nothing significant can be accomplished but by prayer.

Stephen Derbyshire
Lead Pastor
City Gates Church

***

The extraordinary events of the summer of 2017 at City Gates gave birth to a movement of prayer. Over a hundred church members mobilised to join together to seek God, motivated by a compassion for people and the inspiration of the Holy Spirit. Rather than fizzling out after God moved powerfully in answer to specific prayer, many felt even further called to carry on; to climb the mountain of prayer and become a movement. In this book Bunmi tells the story of how it started, combined with compassion for the nation, the conviction of the Holy Spirit to pray and the passion in the heart of all those involved.

This is not a movement that belongs to us or an institution. It belongs to God and this book is designed to inspire others to join together in prayer, provide practical tools and encouragement. A phrase, borrowed from relay races, was used in the early days of this movement. It echoes at the heart of this book, 'passing the baton.' Will you take up the baton of prayer?

Gareth Sherwood
Pastor, Elim Pentecostal Church

TABLE OF CONTENTS

Dedication i

Acknowledgements ii

Foreword v

Introduction 1

Chapter 1: The Tipping Point 5

Chapter 2: The Tower of Prayer is Born 10

Chapter 3: Our Experience to Date 18

Chapter 4: Not by Power or by Might 27

Chapter 5: The Power of Unity 33

Chapter 6: Critical Success Factors 38

Chapter 7: Conclusion 46

Afterword 51

Appendix: The Quick Start Toolkit 54

    Sample Prayer Rota 55

    Sample Fasting Rota 57

    Role of the Overseer 58

    Role of the Administrator 60

    Sample Prayers 61

    Sample Guidelines 68

INTRODUCTION

This book is a call to prayer. These are difficult and perilous times and Christianity is under constant attack. In the midst of the onslaught, God is waking His people up to become fervent and constant in pushing back the darkness.

As you turn the pages, you will discover the remarkable story of the revival that is just starting in a local church in east London. You will also find the new methods and strategies of praying without ceasing that God has equipped the church with, particularly in a busy world where it is becoming increasingly difficult to meet physically to pray as often as is needed.

My prayer is that this account of the journey we have just started will be used by God to create a hunger in your heart for more, leading to the manifest glory of God not just in our local churches but in every facet of our nation.

Although I have been a Christian since 1986, looking back over the years, I see now that my prayers in the main were somewhat narrowly focused on my well-

On the Watch

being and that of my loved ones: nuclear and extended family members; friends and their family members; work colleagues as well as my church leaders and members. I also regularly prayed for the salvation of any unsaved loved ones. I would of course remember to pray for our nation and its leaders as instructed in the book of Timothy; however if I would be honest, those broader prayers for the nation were infrequent, brief and did not have the same passion and fervency as any of my other prayers. It was not that I did not care; I just found it a tad tedious hence praying along those lines often felt like a tick-box exercise.

That was the status quo until June 2017 when a totally unprecedented series of events occurring just after my fiftieth birthday transformed my prayer life. The follow-on from that chapter of my life is that I now constantly and earnestly pray for the United Kingdom with a fervency that I never had before. Even better, I am not the only one whose prayer life has changed, God has touched the lives of many of us within my local church and He is continuing to do so.

My heart's cry is that as you read this book, you will be transformed by the power of God and:

- The secrets of praying without ceasing will be revealed to you.

Introduction

- Your spiritual eyes will be enlightened to understand the times and seasons that we are currently living in.
- You will be filled with both holy anger and compassion at the same time regarding the spiritual state of our nation, leading you to fervently pray and become a stronger witness for Christ.
- Faith will arise in you to believe God for the fire of His revival to spread across your community and nation.
- You will discover how to pray more effectively as an individual and also corporately with other church members.
- You will start or become part of an effective bible-based prayer group that remains constant in prayer, bringing about change in our nation.

Chapter 1:

THE TIPPING POINT

It was June 2017 and at City Gates Church we had just completed a three-day period of prayer and fasting. Velveta Thompson, one of our worship leaders had ministered powerfully in one of the prayer sessions between Tuesday and Thursday, however by Sunday afternoon we learnt that she had taken ill the evening before and had been rushed to hospital. To our shock and utter dismay, she went into a coma within a few days of being admitted to the hospital!

The news about the coma broke on 20 June, it was a Tuesday which happened to be the same day as our church's weekly prayer meeting. The timing therefore provided an opportunity for a large group of people to come together to pray for her recovery. The atmosphere in the prayer meeting that evening was electric as most of us were still fired up from the previous week's prayer and fasting period, more so we had seen Velveta pray and worship powerfully during those sessions. One other timing opportunity God provided was that just a few weeks before, Peter Vandenberg of *Christ for All Nations* had visited our church to share the powerful testimony of his miraculous healing from a very aggressive and rare form of cancer; over and over again as he spoke to us, he mentioned that people prayed for him continuously through it all. Against this backdrop we stood together in unity and faith and cried out to God with a sense of urgency.

During the prayer meeting two specific scriptures came to my mind - James 5:16 and Acts 12 – and it occurred to me that if the church prayed **earnestly** like Elijah and **constantly** like the early church, Velveta could be set free from the clutches of death just as Peter had experienced freedom from Herod's death sentence in Acts 12. Pondering upon this further, I recalled that on a separate occasion in the past, a number of us in the church had used Doodle[1] and a WhatsApp group to create a 30-day prayer & fasting chain. I therefore reckoned that it would make sense to employ a similar

---

[1] An online tool used for scheduling

approach in this case.

Although I did not take immediate action that night, I had no peace until I set up the group almost twenty-four hours later on Wednesday 21 June. The prayer chain kicked off at 8pm that day. Working with Bola, a much-trusted sister in Christ, we rolled up our sleeves, scheduled 30-minute prayer slots using Doodle and added a few members of our church to a WhatsApp group specifically created for this purpose. I also posted a message on the group asking members to let anyone else who wanted to join the prayer group get in touch with myself or Bola. We set out to have an unbroken prayer chain for 72 hours with each person in the group praying for 30 minutes before handing over the baton to the next person. This meant we had 144 prayer slots and needed 48 committed people willing to pray for a minimum of 30-minutes daily over a three-day period.

Looking back, it is purely by the grace of God that we were able to organise the group that evolved whilst not feeling overwhelmed or losing sight of our goal. There was a massive wave of unity and faith which meant that as WhatsApp group administrators we were receiving numerous requests day and night from church members who wanted to commit to prayer. With a participation level which doubled our intended population, we nearly broke the back of Doodle since it is not designed for that level of activity. We ended up with about 100 participants selecting from 144 prayer slot options and some of them did not know how to use Doodle. More importantly people prayed earnestly, in unity and in faith and by the Spirit of God the back of the enemy was broken. We set out to have an unbroken prayer chain for 72 hours and to God be all the glory, our dear sister in Christ woke up from the coma mid-afternoon on Saturday 24 June, shortly before the 72-hour mark!

The totally unscripted and phenomenal outcome of this prayer chain can only be God-ordained. It is a classic case of *what the enemy intended for evil, God turned around for good*. The prayer chain caused a revival to begin in our midst. Soon after we started, some of the group's participants began to express the desire to continue beyond the agreed period and as such when Velveta woke up on the third day it was unanimously agreed that we needed to continue praying until she had fully recovered. So we extended it to seven days; and after seven days there was no letting up as yet again the group insisted on continuing until she was back at home. Amazingly, even though we were not meeting together physically to pray, checking the posts on the WhatsApp group often felt like walking into an energised prayer meeting, the community was vibrant and alive in praise, worship and prayer continually.

Some members of the group even described themselves as prayer addicts – what an awesome place to be – we could not stop praying and to God be the glory, we received what we asked for in His name. Velveta is alive and well today and we had a thanksgiving service to celebrate her healing on Sunday 13 August, eight weeks after she went into hospital.

Chapter 2:

THE TOWER OF PRAYER IS BORN

I will call that episode *day one* because with the hand of God clearly upon us something new had been birthed and a revival was starting…

What began as a very alarming incident became the catalyst that gave birth to the start of a spiritual revival in our midst. It brings the following scripture to mind: "But the rulers of this world have not understood it; if they had, they would not have crucified our glorious Lord. That is what the Scriptures mean when they say, 'No eye has seen, no ear has heard, and no mind has imagined what God has prepared for those who love him.'" *1 Corinthians 2:8-9 NLT*

The Mission

During the period when we were praying for Velveta, a few of us began to sense the need to continue the prayer chain not just on an on-going basis but also for a broader purpose. This scripture continued to be impressed upon us: "I have posted watchmen on your walls, Jerusalem; they will never be silent day or night. You who call on the Lord, give yourselves no rest, and give him no rest till he establishes Jerusalem and makes her the praise of the earth" *Isaiah 62:6-7 NIV.*

We therefore agreed that we would continue to focus on praying for Velveta until the thanksgiving service which had been planned to celebrate her healing; and following that celebration we would step into the unfolding vision of becoming watchmen and watchwomen who wait continually upon the Lord to **see His Kingdom come**.

On 14 August we stepped into the new era, *day two* had begun and a new WhatsApp group was created which we aptly titled the watchtower in line with our mandate; more than seventy of our original members opted in. The God-inspired mandate of the prayer group is to **stand guard in unity and prayer as soldiers for Christ** which means we will jointly and continually pray for God's will to be done in the body of Christ, local community, nation and the world at large. In the main we are continually praying along these lines:

- For **those who are unsaved** to come to know Christ: that the body of Christ will show His love and compassion and operate in the demonstration of His power AND many souls will be won to Him as we do so. "Then he said to his disciples, 'The harvest is plentiful but the workers are few. Ask the Lord of the harvest, therefore, to send out workers into his harvest field.'" *Matthew 9:37-38 NIV*

- For the **healing of our land** and for every agenda of the enemy against the body of Christ to be aborted i.e. uprooting and pulling down every false ideology, false religion, rise in immorality, violence or crime and everything that is not of God in our land: "if my people, who are called by my name, will humble themselves and pray and seek my face and turn from their wicked ways, then I will hear from heaven, and I will forgive their sin and will heal their land."*2 Chronicles 7:14 NIV*

- For the Church to **take back what has been lost**; to be the salt and light and become influential in the land again by establishing institutions such as schools and hospitals that are centres of excellence. We want to see these institutions feeding spirit, soul and body

The Tower of Prayer is Born

in a wholesome manner in line with the Word of God and leading many to Christ in the process. *"Jesus said, 'Let the little children come to me, and do not hinder them, for the kingdom of heaven belongs to such as these.'" Matthew 19:14 NIV*

We have been praying along these lines as led by the Holy Spirit since 14 August 2017. However little did we know when we started back then that as soon as schools resumed in September, there would be a barrage of fiery darts, assaults and persecution targeted at Christian parents and teachers stemming from the increased promotion of ideologies opposed to the teachings of Christ. We are living in disturbing times and there is an overwhelming body of evidence of the blatantly depraved state of our nation being displayed on a daily basis which compels us to pray earnestly. The way the Christian voice is increasingly being silenced is very alarming. There seems to be a deliberate attempt to infiltrate the hearts and minds of the young with utter darkness and we are at risk of the next and future generations not having any idea of the biblical truths of right and wrong.

The watchtower exists because we believe that sons and daughters of the Most High God need to take a spiritual stand against the strangulating tirade of evil and fight for our souls and the souls of the upcoming generations. In the watchtower we have chosen to do this in the place of compassionate prayer for the lost until we see His Kingdom come.

The Church has been asleep for too long and this is a wake up call to arise from slumber and take our rightful place as salt and light. We need to battle spiritually, recognising that we have the authority to do so in Jesus name:

- "For though we live in the world, we do not wage war as the world does. The weapons we fight with are not the weapons of the world. On the contrary, they have divine power to demolish strongholds." *2 Corinthians 10:3-4 NIV*
- "For our struggle is not against flesh and blood, but against the rulers, against the authorities, against the powers of this dark world and against the spiritual forces of evil in the heavenly realms." *Ephesians 6:12 NIV*

How we operate

The watchtower is a place of continuous praise, worship and prayer that has a pleasantly surprising vibrancy especially when you consider that our meeting place is on a WhatsApp forum. Despite being a virtual prayer meeting, the presence of God is palpable and it often feels like you have walked into a physical prayer room when you join in. Quite often

The Tower of Prayer is Born

we see very engaging posts when participants start to pray. These posts range from *I'm praying in the tower now* to *I'm ascending the tower; I'm on the watch now; I'm joining the tower of praise and worship* and so on. Members of the group are at liberty under the guidance of the Holy Spirit to post prayers, worship songs, words of encouragement and inspirational bible verses to the group at any time in line with the broad prayer themes articulated above. It is a great delight to witness an overflow of the Spirit of God for the edification of the body on a daily basis; which is effectively a twenty-first century manifestation of the scripture which says: "Let the message of Christ dwell among you richly as you teach and admonish one another with all wisdom through psalms, hymns, and songs from the Spirit, singing to God with gratitude in your hearts." *Colossians 3:16 NIV*

Each day is split into eight distinct three-hour prayer-watch periods (watches) starting from 12 midnight. At least two people pray within each watch however for the very popular time slots we have as many as eight people praying in a watch. We also have an average of two people fasting every day. Given that we have more than 70 participants, each member of the group only commits to fast one day a month unless they prefer to do more. For transparency and to ensure we have all watches covered, we maintain a

On the Watch

central timetable so we know who to expect in the watchtower and when. We however have such a good blend of commitment and flexibility that we often find people joining in to pray more times than they have committed to. One of the heart-warming things about this group is that although participation is voluntary and nothing is forced upon anyone, members are very committed to the cause and the fact that they have caught the vision is very evident from the vibrant participation and enthusiasm levels. This can only be because God is the driver of the group and He is steering it in the direction He wants it to go.

Fourteen overseers including two administrators lead the group. This level of oversight has proven to be effective as it helps with accountability whilst ensuring that none of the leaders feel overburdened. They operate as servant leaders facilitating the smooth running of the watchtower. Each prayer watch is covered by an overseer who is responsible for posting a summary of the key prayer points at the start of the watch. The overseer also helps keep the sense of community by making people feel welcome when they post to the watchtower to confirm they have joined and are praying.

About once or twice a week, the administrators, supported by the overseers post more detailed prayer points to the group as led by the Holy Spirit. These

The Tower of Prayer is Born

additional prayer points provide specific or further insights into how to pray earnestly about some or all the main prayer themes of the watchtower outlined earlier. Typically these are influenced by trends in the news, prompts from the church's leadership or from other members of the group. A recent example is where we have been praying for fellow Christians in the UK who are being persecuted for their faith and/or are being bullied out of office because they have chosen to stand upon biblical truths and not deny Christ.

In addition to the above, we regularly cover healing prayer points for any member of the group or their immediate family members who may be ill.

Chapter 3:

OUR EXPERIENCE TO DATE

The revival is just beginning and God has been pleasantly surprising us since it started. What you are reading now is the start of the journey; my prayer is that the fire God has ignited amongst us will spread across our nation and we will see many more supernatural signs and wonders in our land as others in the body of Christ join in to battle for the land.

Our individual and collective prayer-lives have most certainly changed for the better and with that comes a deeper knowledge of Him as well as being equipped with everything we require for living a godly life. Prayer has become a habit for the members of the group, not in a robotic or mechanical manner but people find themselves fulfilling the command to "pray without ceasing," *1 Thessalonians 5:17 NKJV* due to a heightened God-consciousness. We also find that with no compulsion whatsoever, a good number of participants continue to keep to their commitment to pray for our nation even when on holidays albeit sometimes with a revised time slot due to time zone differences.

There is a change in our wider church services with a greater demonstration of the power of the Holy Spirit during worship and prayer meetings accompanied by more souls being saved, and visions and prophetic words of wisdom being revealed.

A recent breakthrough we have experienced is that the Gideons Bible Society has been able to give a thousand bibles to pupils in our local area in just one school term. In one of the schools, every pupil opted in to receive a bible. Doors that were previously closed are now open - a school they had tried to reach with no positive outcome for over ten years has now opened its doors, with their pupils receiving almost two hundred bibles.

We have been praying constantly for the Gideons Bible Society on the watchtower and this is clearly an answer to prayer. We are continuing to pray that more doors will be open and the word of God will

On the Watch

come alive in the pupils as they go through the pages of the bibles they have received.

The watchtower has not been without its own challenges. We have noticed that similar to the battle the Israelites had with the Amalekites in Exodus 17, there is a direct correlation between the level of prayer cover for the group and the level of participation of its members. The more the group is lifted up in prayer, the more fervent we all are in the place of prayer. Opportunities to become distracted are rife; levels of participation start to dwindle rapidly any time we take our eyes off the ball even if just momentarily.

One example of how the enemy has tried to derail us is through sickness. Soon after we started praying together some members of the group began to suffer from ill health, however because we are fighting from the point of victory we have continuously experienced the healing power of our Lord Jesus. Furthermore God has helped us to see how these incidents are opportunities to develop more as an army. We have found that such attacks make everyone more resolute to stand guard together in unity to defend our fellow warriors and pursue the vision God has laid upon our hearts. Our trust is in God that as a group we will continue to be soaked in His anointing and presence such that we are always several steps ahead of any ploys to distract or derail us thus proactively quenching them before they arise.

Despite these successes, we are not resting on our laurels, we are continually praying that the fire of the revival that has started in our midst will continue to burn brightly not just in our local church but in every church in our land and as we continue to do so we will see our nation return to the Lord and His kingdom established.

Testimonies from the watchtower

The revelations we have had whilst setting up and running the watchtower have been amazing. One of them occurred through the practical parable of Velveta's healing described in this book. The Lord wants us as Christians to see the lost as dear loved ones who are terminally ill or dying. Are we bothered enough to help make a difference - to change the prognosis, save their lives or their souls?

Many of us have had the news that someone we love so dearly is dying. We know the pain and stifling helplessness – feeling that we are powerless to change things. If *all we do*, is get busy and work very hard at: taking them food and fresh clothing to change into; getting bigger and better rooms in the hospital; sitting by their bedside; making them smile; letting them know we are there etc., then unfortunately we are still just waiting for them to die. If however in addition to doing these things we get on our knees and ask the Creator of all things to intervene and we ask fervently without ceasing as He (our God) has asked us to, then we tap into a greater strength than ours – into the only real power that we have as Christians.

The watchtower is like a church's prayer arm - the power generator of the programmes designed to reach the lost, the community and the nation. The unsaved are terminally ill spiritually, dying right before our eyes. Yes, we have to visit, put on events to engage them, share the gospel, but the real game changer is the power of non-stop collective prayer - people praying with a heart that is breaking and depending primarily on the supernatural power of the Holy Spirit.

No church should be without such a prayer arm.

- Bola Abiloye

The watchtower prayer group at City Gates started out of a painful experience in our church, when a wonderful sister was unexpectedly struck down with serious illness. A round-the-clock prayer chain was started and this continued until our sister was fully recovered. After this, the leaders and some members of the prayer group felt the Lord was calling us to have an on-going prayer chain, members enthusiastically signed up to join, and since then we have had testimonies of answered prayers.

My experience from this is the revival of my prayer life and the passion that I have developed for things that matter to the Kingdom. During this short time, the Holy Spirit has emphasised to me that prayer is the divinely ordained strategy that leads us to the power and victory of Christ; Satan knows we will remain defeated without it. Praying is the last thing that Satan wants you to do therefore do not underestimate the power of prayer.

"And they overcame him by the blood of the Lamb and by the word of their testimony, and they did not love their lives to the death." *Revelation 12:11 NKJV*

"Again I say to you that if two of you agree on earth concerning anything that they ask, it will be done for them by My Father in heaven. For where two or three are gathered together in My name, I am there in the midst of them." *Matthew 18:19-20 NKJV*

- Robert Quaye

The start of the watchtower was the beginning of something that I never imagined would have such a great impact on me personally and the church. It heightened my ability to hear from the Lord and I saw how He beautifully confirmed what He was saying through others on the watchtower. It increased my love and compassion for the lost and the urgency of the church to have an impact on our community.

I remember sending a WhatsApp message to the prayer leaders seven days after the WhatsApp group was set up for 24/7 prayer cover for Velveta saying that I sensed the Lord was saying that this level of prayer should continue even after Velveta is completely healed. I went on to say that this continuous prayer needs to cover the body of Christ and our community for us to see God's purpose established, people from all walks of life saved and the body of Christ functioning as the Lord intended. Isaiah 62: 6-7 which refers to posting watchmen on the wall and praying night and day came to mind.

Little did I know at the time that the Lord was laying this on the hearts of others as well. I can now see that the Lord in His sovereignty and power was building and strengthening His church in a way I would never have perceived. This whole journey has reminded me of the battle that we are engaging in and the importance of unity within the body of Christ. I feel humbled and sober to be part of such an amazing journey with my brothers and sisters and I believe this is just the beginning of something greater in reaching the lost and establishing God's kingdom.

- Samantha Trimmer

Our Experience to Date

My experience on the watchtower so far has been good. God has moved me from inadequacy to capability. I recall telling some of the team members that I never considered myself a prayer warrior. I had other gifts such as singing but I did not see prayer as one of my strengths. I remember sending a text to one of the leaders of the group asking if she heard about Velveta in hospital; days later she sent me a text stating that she had started a WhatsApp prayer chain for Velveta's healing and had added me. Looking back, I thank God that she didn't ask me otherwise I would have hesitated. Rather I felt at the time that if she had added me it must be that she was led by God to do so. I am most certainly grateful to God for her obedience.

So the journey began... I was led by the Holy Spirit to be free on the group, nothing holding me back, just free to pray and worship. It blessed me when I posted a worship song and someone replied to say they had just sang it at home group. I knew we were on the same wavelength.

The watchtower has been a blessing as we have seen others receiving their healing. Also it is good to see the eagerness and commitment of the members who step in to pray even when it is not their assigned prayer time.

Overall, I feel the watchtower is a great prayer tool to

On the Watch

intercede for one another, our community and our nation. I know my prayer life has improved as a result.

- Josie Nwaelene

Chapter 4:

NOT BY POWER OR BY MIGHT

My heart's desire is to see this powerful phenomenon replicated in every church across our nation and indeed throughout the world as it is in the place of prayer that we will receive the power, wisdom and insightful strategies to push back the spiritual darkness which seems to be encroaching upon us in these end times.

The watchtower started under the guidance of the Spirit of God and it remains on track because we are continuing in obedience to Him. My prayer is that as you read this book, you will receive power and direction from the King of kings coupled with the boldness to step out in faith and team up with fellow Christians in your local church whose hearts He has prepared to continuously pray for the nation. I strongly believe that as we stand watch together in the powerful name of Jesus, we will see His kingdom come and His glory fill the earth.

I am reminded of the widow in *2 Kings 4* who cried out to Elisha and experienced the miracle of multiplication as she poured out her small jar of oil into empty vessels. We understand that the flow of oil continued until there were no more vessels to receive the oil. Our watchtower experience to date shows that God is ready to pour out His anointing upon His children for the manifestation of His glory all across our nation. The question is, are there enough willing vessels available and ready to be filled for service?

God is looking for those who will come as they are with no other agenda than to serve Him faithfully in spirit and in truth. It is remarkable to note that neither the church's leadership nor the leaders of the group coerced anyone to join the watchtower; once we concluded praying for Velveta, those who chose to continue actively opted-in based on their inner conviction as led by the Holy Spirit and the word of God.

The truly voluntary nature of this group of people who are not compelled by anyone but by God, heavily influences how we operate. In the watchtower we do not come to the battlefront in our own power -

Not by Power or by Might

we would have grown weary if we did so. We constantly cover one another in prayer so that we will not be derailed, we will not become lukewarm and we will not be distracted. We do not come to the place of prayer warfare with a judgemental spirit, we come with our hearts bleeding for the lost and with a desire to see His kingdom come; we are continually asking Him to break our hearts with the things that break His heart.

We do not come to seek the Lord's face because we are better than others, we come because we are also flawed but saved by grace and we want to see that same grace freely received by everyone around us. We know we have an advocate in Jesus and that we can always come to Him for the forgiveness of our sins but we are conscious that the *accuser of the brethren* would rather we did not know our place in Jesus; hence we do not to give room to the enemy, instead we rely on Jesus constantly to set us apart and consecrate us for His service.

The cry for our nation in prayer draws each of us even closer to Jesus. We recognise that we are powerless without Him and that we overcome in His name however our prayers are not mere chants of His name otherwise we would be beaten up like the sons of Sceva in *Acts 19*. Rather we draw close to Him because we have a relationship with Him and as we do so humbly with our lives surrendered to Him, He gives us the battle strategy to effectively push back the darkness from our nation. We exercise authority in His name not because of our own righteousness but because the saving blood of our Lord Jesus gives us boldness to sit in heavenly places with Him.

We are often tempted to despair but we recall that in *1 Kings 18* whilst Elijah thought he was all alone, Obadiah had hidden one hundred other prophets who had remained faithful to the Lord. We recognise in the watchtower that we are not fighting flesh and blood hence we put on the full armour of God daily as outlined in *Ephesians 6*. To take our nation back for the Lord Jesus we need full reliance on Him as we cannot do it in our own strength. As aptly stated by the early twentieth century Scottish minster, Oswald Chambers: "We have to pray with our eyes on God, not on the difficulties".

We do not operate in fear because like the Apostles when we pray, we are filled with boldness. "After this prayer, the meeting place shook, and they were all filled with the Holy Spirit. Then they preached the word of God with boldness." *Acts 4:31 NLT*

We do not count ourselves to have arrived because like Paul, we are pressing on; we know the harvest is vast as the Lord has opened our eyes to see what is at stake. "Brothers and sisters, I do not consider myself yet to have taken hold of it. But one thing I do: Forgetting what is behind and straining toward what is ahead," *Philippians 3:13 NIV*

We do not feel overwhelmed by the task at hand; we remain in the place of prayer irrespective of the news we hear on a daily basis because we always lift up the name of Jesus and we know that as we praise Him, the Lion of the tribe of Judah will throw confusion into the camp of the dark forces just as He did when Jehoshaphat was king of Judah. "As they began to sing and praise, the Lord set ambushes against the men of Ammon and Moab and Mount Seir who were invading Judah, and they were defeated. The Ammonites and Moabites rose up against the men from Mount Seir to destroy and annihilate them. After they finished slaughtering the men from Seir, they helped to destroy one another." *2 Chronicles 20:22-23 NIV*

We stay strong and focused because we depend on the same God who spoke to Zerubbabel: "So he said to me, "This is the word of the LORD to Zerubbabel: 'Not by might nor by power, but by my Spirit,' says the LORD Almighty." *Zechariah 4:6 NIV*

Andrew Murray, one of the champions of the South African revival in the nineteenth century is known to

On the Watch

have said: "The man who mobilises the Christian church to pray will make the greatest contribution to world evangelisation in history." Perhaps you are reading this book today because you are one of the vessels the Lord wants to fill with His oil for service or maybe you are one of the prophets in hiding that needs to come out and join in the spiritual battle. Why not take a moment to pause, ponder and pray about this...

Chapter 5:

THE POWER OF UNITY

In the Old Testament story often dubbed the *Tower of Babel* we see that God said the people who wanted to build the tower could not be stopped unless their language became confused and they were no longer united.

""Look!" he said. "The people are united, and they all speak the same language. After this, nothing they set out to do will be impossible for them!"" *Genesis 11:6 NLT*

Since God Himself spoke these words, I do not think it can be any clearer that unity is really a formidable force and its power cannot be overstated. Jesus also confirmed the converse in the New Testament - the consequence of disunity: "If a house is divided against itself, that house cannot stand." *Mark 3:25 NIV*

Unfortunately, the church has been a *divided house* for too long. In my opinion, one of the reasons why there is such an onslaught against the body of Christ today is that whilst the church has been split into several ineffective splinters, fighting against each other rather than collectively fighting the common enemy; the enemy has spent the time planting weeds amongst us. He has been strengthening the forces of darkness to collectively speak with one voice against the very foundations of our existence. However we serve an all-powerful God and it is not too late for the church to arise in strength and in the assurance of the word of God, "But you belong to God, my dear children. You have already won a victory over those people, because the Spirit who lives in you is greater than the spirit who lives in the world." *1 John 4:4 NLT*

Beyond a shadow of doubt, I am convinced that if the people of God unite in the place of prayer, we will be able to powerfully demolish the strongholds of the enemy against our nation. It is time to hear the clarion call, bury the hatchet, forget our dividing denominational badges and work together to push back the spiritual darkness and advance the kingdom of God for this generation and generations to come.

One Purpose, Different Expressions

One of the reasons why the watchtower has been continuing successfully is that its members are focused on the vision from a place of unity. We are a diverse group with different approaches to prayer. Whilst some like to spend more time in worship, there are others who prefer to spend more time in prayer; whilst some prefer to spend more time praying with their understanding, there are others who prefer to spend more time praying in tongues; whilst some like to post lengthy prayers to the chat group, others would merely post *praying now* and leave it at that. No one focuses on one method being better than the other as long as everything is done in line with the word of God. Rather we continue to trust the Holy Spirit to guide us and we move forward as one army for the Lord. I have certainly learnt some excellent ways of praying that I had never explored before. We have experienced times where someone declares via the chat group that they feel led to fast and pray more intently for a particular issue within our main themes and because some others within the group have the same conviction, they join in whether or not they were scheduled to pray that day. Neither those who explicitly join in when such calls are made nor those who do not are more spiritual or superior; what is most important is that we remain all focused on the mission at hand and press on towards our common goal which is to see His kingdom come. We have the *one purpose* view that the Apostle Paul spoke about, "I planted the seed, Apollos watered it, but God has been making it grow. So neither the one who plants nor the one who waters is anything, but only God, who makes things grow. The one who plants and the one who waters have one purpose, and they will each be rewarded according to their own labor." *1 Corinthians 3:6-8 NIV*

How marvellous and powerful would it be if all across the United Kingdom, we had numerous Christians standing together in the place of prayer, irrespective of denomination, for the same purpose: to see our nation return to God and to see His kingdom come? The story is told in the book of Esther of how the Jews came together to fast and pray when a death sentence was pronounced upon them. Dare I say that we are in a similar situation, at the verge of a death sentence being pronounced upon life based on biblical principles, as we know it? We however know that the death sentence levied against the Jews was reversed in the place of prayer. For this reason we also are sure of victory, for the gates of hell will not prevail against the kingdom of God. The first step though is to stand together in the place of prayer for it is as we unite in prayer, praise and worship that the anointing is released and we become more effective. "How good and pleasant it is when God's people live together in unity! It is like precious oil poured on the head, running down on the beard, running down on Aaron's beard, down on the collar of his robe. It is as if the dew of Hermon were falling on Mount Zion. For there the Lord bestows his blessing, even life forevermore." *Psalm 133: 1-3 NIV*

Are you ready to forget trivial differences and focus on joining forces with the rest of the body of Christ to push back the spiritual darkness and advance the kingdom of God in our nation?

Chapter 6:

CRITICAL SUCCESS FACTORS

I am amazed at how we have continued this journey and my prayer is that we will be empowered by the Holy Spirit to remain faithful to the end without wavering. God has given us the wisdom to operate in some practical ways that enable us to stay focused and constant in prayer.

Staying Focused

It is important to recognise first and foremost that our motivation as a group is compassion for the unsaved. The prayer group neither has a political agenda nor is it a hate group. Our focus is not on whether the nation should leave or remain in Europe or whether Scotland should remain or leave the UK. We do not exist to target anyone because of his or her ideologies, beliefs or anything else. Rather our battle is spiritual; our focus is for God's will to be done, for His Kingdom to come and for His name to be the praise of the earth.

The group is not a gossip or scare-mongering forum hence prayer points are kept at a high level to discourage fake news, unnecessary tongue wagging and exaggeration but with enough detail to help us pray effectively. We encourage those who are baptised in the Spirit and have a prayer language to also pray in tongues during their watch period where possible, as God knows every detail of what we need to pray for. "In the same way, the Spirit helps us in our weakness. We do not know what we ought to pray for, but the Spirit himself intercedes for us through wordless groans. And he who searches our hearts knows the mind of the Spirit, because the Spirit intercedes for God's people in accordance with the will of God." *Romans 8:26-27 NIV*

One other thing that keeps the watchtower on track is that it operates more like a special purpose vehicle; it has a very specific mission and therefore complements but does not replace the church's regular prayer ministry or intercessory team. Having this clear distinction means that we are able to stay focused on the mission: *not to rest and to give God no rest until we see*

On the Watch

His kingdom established in the context of seeing our nation turn back to God. The demarcation helps guarantee that watchtower prayer points are not pushed to the back burner as a result of having several other requests. What this means in practice is that where prayer points outside of the main watchtower themes are raised, we ask the regular prayer ministry or intercessors team to take them on. It does not mean we do not care about these other requests or that members do not pray about them, what it ensures is that the dedicated 30-minute slot that each person has committed to, specifically covers the main prayer themes. Incidentally a good number of the saints in the watchtower also belong to the other prayer teams in church so they often cover the additional prayer points via those other groups. An exception to this rule is when we have what we call *wounded soldier* situations; this is where anyone in the watchtower or their immediate family member is ill. We stand guard together as a group to pray for them alongside our main prayer points as we recognise that we need to form a defence for each other in the battlefront so that we can continue to engage effectively together in combat.

We have some guidelines, some of which are highlighted below, to help us stay on point and guard against the WhatsApp forum being abused or

Critical Success Factors

used for abuse:

Members are encouraged to post their prayers to the chat group at any time using their own original words and /or direct quotes from the bible bearing in mind that our warfare is from a place of compassion. Inflammatory language is therefore not used on the group and we do not speak negatively of anyone or any groups of people; rather we pray for the light of God's word to shine into everyone's heart, ours included.

For example we pray:

- For forgiveness for every form of sexual immorality;
- For God to open the eyes of people with confused identity;
- For God to forgive those trying to confuse others;
- For God to reveal the error of their ways to those trying to confuse others;
- For God to open the eyes of anyone bound by false beliefs or ideologies;
- That we will respond to everyone as Jesus expects us to, with love and sound teaching.

Links to news items of any nature are not forwarded to the group, rather if a member believes that any

On the Watch

news item falls under the watchtower's main prayer themes then they explain the point and rephrase it as a prayer point in their own words. This helps us to steer clear of sensationalism of any kind.

Chain chats, texts, pictures, videos or viral greetings such as Happy New Day / Happy Weekend / Happy New Month and so on are not forwarded to the group. This ensures we do not clog up each other's phones or derail each other from keeping the main thing the main thing.

This section cannot be concluded without highlighting the importance of the rhythmic nature of the battle strategy; it simply cannot be overemphasised. Members have a framework that is reliable; they know what to expect and when to expect it: days are split evenly into three-hour watches, there is clarity about who is praying and fasting and when it is happening. The overseers consistently extend a warm welcome when people arrive on the watchtower, be it day or night, and post a summary of the key prayer points within each watch and so on. Operating in this context helps to keep members focused on the mission and empowers them to self-manage without needing to expend undue energy working through uncertainties or chaos.

Staying Constant

A few years ago I signed up to a prayer chain initiative with a number of other Christians. It meant I had to take on the mantle of prayer at 10pm once a week however to my shame I must confess that I struggled at the time and was not as faithful as I would have wanted to be. On hindsight I think I may not have been the only one who dropped out because the initiative fizzled out after a while with no official communication announcing its end; we all just knew it was over!

As much as we all want to do the right thing and remain faithful, a level of accountability helps to nudge us along. My observation is that the framework for the watchtower, which the Lord has helped us to design, facilitates accountability and this is a strong contributing factor to the constancy of the watchtower members.

By design each member is encouraged to commit to a minimum of two 30-minute prayer slots a week and indicate to the group when they start their slot by posting 'praying now' or something to that effect. The main reason for this is not to track members in a legalistic manner but to ensure we keep the platform vibrant and alive given that it is a virtual meeting place. It is also one of the reasons why we have overseers; they make those praying during the period feel welcome. What transpires however is that what you may call 'checking in' when a member starts praying actually serves a dual purpose: it keeps the forum active and at the same time keeps each member accountable. Apart from the occasional nudge, members tend to show up without any additional prompt from the overseers. The transparency of the prayer chain facilitates self-managing behaviour and members feel jointly responsible for the group. You sometimes find people apologising on the forum for missing their prayer slot without anyone hounding or chasing them – there is really a spirit of unity in operation due to the openness, more so as we continually rely on the Holy Spirit.

One other thing that keeps us going is the variety of prayers. Let's face it, praying for broad themes like the nation could be daunting or even tedious however having fellow brothers and sisters who regularly post their Spirit-led prayers to the group means we never run out of ideas and collectively we stand to gain more insight into how to pray, making us better equipped to press on in prayer continuously and passionately.

Another driver for staying constant in the place of prayer is the flexibility built into how we operate. Members pray for 30 minutes at any point during their 3-hour prayer watch; this means they do not have to abandon praying during that watch, if, due to unforeseen events, they were unable to start at an exact time, for instance as a result of delays due to finishing late from work and so on. Those in the 6-9pm watch for example are able to start praying as early as 6pm or as late as 8:30pm. We also find that because there is freedom, people are more open to the Holy Spirit and it is not unusual to find members indicating that they are spending time praying at other times in addition to or instead of their regular slots. Therefore even though things sometimes need to move around slightly in our respective schedules, we continue to experience constant prayer, committed hearts, collective responsibility and open communication.

Chapter 7:

CONCLUSION

Given the current state of our nation, I am convinced that we are on the verge of a revival and God is stirring up His people in the place of prayer to be facilitators for His mighty move. The bible confirms this, "For his anger lasts only a moment, but his favor lasts a lifetime! Weeping may last through the night, but joy comes with the morning." *Psalm 30:5 NLT*. A new day is about to break and it is time for sons and daughters of the Most High God to actively sign up for His move that is currently gathering momentum. More than ever we need to cry out for the salvation of our children, our grandchildren and generations to come. My prayer is that the legacy of this generation of Christians will be that we lifted the banner of Jesus up effectively and so high that it

Conclusion

stopped darkness from engulfing our nation.

The watchtower at City Gates Church started and continues in faith and by the Spirit of God. The reason why we remain in strength and power is that we are united and constantly stay open to His leadings. As this is not a physical battle we are completely reliant on God for strategy and direction. A fantastic by-product is that we find our hearts continually surrendered to Him, which is the best place to be as there is nothing better than the presence of God. Almost every one of us has a regular 9am to 5pm job (longer hours in a lot of cases) nevertheless we are sustained by His grace to continue to pray earnestly and constantly because of the oneness, amazing team spirit and hearts willing to serve. My prayer is that we will continue in unity, strength and in the power of the Holy Spirit.

As with every worthwhile venture, we have had our share of challenges. However the good news is that we are battling from a position of victory, so we have overcome and will continue to overcome because our reliance is on the All-wise, All-sufficient, All-knowing and All-powerful God. Every challenge faced draws the group closer together and closer to Jesus, which makes us stronger and more determined to see a spiritual revival in our land. The rewards are enormous, the spiritual growth and boldness that come with stepping out in alignment with His will are astounding. God is indeed faithful and He is a rewarder of those that diligently seek Him. My prayer is that we will continue to trust Him to overcome every fiery dart and that we will become even more formidable in Him.

At City Gates Church, the altar of continuous prayer started according to the will of God. We saw the hand of God move through a prayer chain that was initiated because we wanted God to save a loved one from the clutches of death; receiving that miracle made us realise He expects us to cry out to Him with the same fervency for the lost all across our nation.

The Lord has opened our eyes to see that despite the busy-ness of this present age, we can make the most of modern technology and social media to push back the darkness and advance His kingdom. This is an irony, as most people on the watchtower would admit that hitherto social media was an object of distraction.

People opted in to the watchtower, not because they were guilt tripped into signing up but because the Holy Spirit revealed to us individually and collectively the need to cry out for our nation in prayer. We are grateful to God that when He looked for willing vessels, He found and chose to use us. The lives of all those involved in this journey have been transformed. However this is just the beginning and there is no reason why the fire of continuous prayer that has

Conclusion

started amongst us cannot be replicated by being lit up and down our nation from east to west and from north to south. What a powerful phenomenon that would be to the glory of God! As you conclude reading this book consider these questions:

- Are you tired of hearing in the news on a daily basis how depraved the society has become?
- Do you care that so many have been deceived and opportunities for hearing and responding to the gospel are steadily being squeezed out?
- Are you concerned about the kind of world that the next generation will be brought up in?
- Do you want to be a part of the solution?

If you have answered *yes* to some or all of these questions, then:

- Are you willing to be engaged in spiritual battle for the revival of our nation?
- Will you hear the heartbeat of the Father and respond by stepping out in faith?
- Will you prayerfully consider reaching out to others in your local church to start a group that prays without ceasing for our nation?

It is my prayer that this book has encouraged you to believe that we will see the hand of God move in our nation if we love the lost enough to constantly cry out

On the Watch

for their salvation; and motivated you to take this journey with us.

Should you require further practical guidance on how to set up a similar group in your local church, we can be contacted by email: info@theprayertower.com; face-to-face coaching can also be scheduled by prior arrangement. May the Lord bless you as you take your position for His kingdom.

AFTERWORD

The incredible journey travelled by Velveta and I, along with our daughters and son-in-law was a very unusual one where we had no time to *pack, prepare and get ready* for a journey along the darkest lanes, lonely roads and what at times appeared to be a cul-de-sac.

From feeling sick after attending a birthday celebration, ministering in song by request; within 24 hours Velveta's body was attacked with what was eventually diagnosed as meningitis, pneumonia on both lungs and micro haemorrhages on the brain. We would not have believed it if a prophetic word had alerted us to the fight of our lives we were about to face. Within a few days of being admitted to the hospital, Velveta was in a coma.

As she lay motionless on the hospital bed, like with many others in this situation, the enemy threw everything at us, mainly attacking our inner thoughts and faith. For me, the worst moments were the first few nights when I would come home from the hospital. However, within a few days, after sending out a few more prayer requests to friends all over the world, I along with the family moved into 'intercessory praise, prayer and worship'. In particular, we are thankful to a prayer group based in our local church, which later became the watchtower. They swiftly organised a round-the-clock prayer vigil for Velveta.

To be honest, I thought I understood the principles of 'intercessory worship' having ministered on many occasions at meetings facilitated by powerful intercessors. But, there is something different about **fighting a personal fight** on behalf of your wife or someone close. It is interesting how during these moments and seasons, the Holy Spirit reminds you of particular scriptures that are poignant for the time.

Even whilst the medical team gave us their daily report and prognosis, we continued praying and worshipping over Velveta. On the second day in the CCU, I already started planning a thanksgiving service believing that God would wake her out of the coma.

When one commits to prayer and fasting, I believe there must be an emphasis on the preparation. Just like if you are preparing a three-course meal, much thought and preparation would go into the ingredients, flavours and cooking conditions. Additionally, it is also very important that the diners are expectant and have a healthy appetite.

I noticed how strategically the Lord selected the

prayer-partners who kicked off the prayer vigil, how united and committed these individuals were to the mission at hand as the Lord had been preparing them for the battle ahead of that moment.

It is quite evident how compassionate and loving these individuals are in general. What better people could we have hoped for to commit themselves to praying for my wife? Just like Jesus was always moved by compassion before he healed the sick and the destitute, I am convinced and convicted that our prayers must be fuelled by an expectant heart towards the Father coupled with care, love and compassion for those we intend to pray for.

The watchtower, I believe under the guidance of the Holy Spirit, received a download from Heaven reminding us of the prayer model Jesus taught us through His word. ***When you pray...***

Velveta and I are eternally thankful that God chose us to travel this arduous journey with the watchtower. May we all become watchful individuals, anticipating the return of our Lord, but also fulfilling the mandate of every believer and that is to partake in and of the ministry of Jesus - standing in the gap and mediating on behalf of our brothers and sisters.

- Steve Thompson
Director - Beracahmusic Ministries International

Appendix

THE QUICK START TOOLKIT

You will find in this section some examples of the templates used for the watchtower at City Gates Church; additionally some of the detailed prayers that overseers have posted to the group and the broad guidelines we follow are included.

We have found these templates and guidelines to be effective to date and my expectation is that these examples will help you get a similar prayer group off the ground in your church. However these examples are not intended to be prescriptive, rather they constitute a framework which you can adapt as you deem fit under the guidance of the Holy Spirit and bearing in mind the context of your own church.

Additional examples can be found at our website: www.theprayertower.com

SAMPLE PRAYER ROTA

This template is based on our expected minimum participation which is for there to be at least two people praying within each three-hour watch period. Each person commits to pray for 30-minutes. In our experience, we have more than two people praying in most watches.

Daily	Mon	Tue	Wed	Thu	Fri	Sat	Sun
Overseer							
00:00-03:00							
00:00-03:00							
Overseer							
03:00-06:00							
03:00-06:00							
Overseer							
06:00-09:00							
06:00-09:00							
Overseer							
09:00-12:00							
09:00-12:00							
Overseer							
12:00-15:00							
12:00-15:00							
Overseer							
15:00-18:00							
15:00-18:00							

Overseer							
18:00-21:00							
18:00-21:00							
Overseer							
21:00-00:00							
21:00-00:00							

SAMPLE FASTING ROTA

This template is based on our expected minimum participation which is for there to be at least two people fasting each day.

4-weeks	Mon	Tue	Wed	Thu	Fri	Sat	Sun
Week 1	01-Jan	02-Jan	03-Jan	04-Jan	05-Jan	06-Jan	07-Jan
Week 2	08-Jan	09-Jan	10-Jan	11-Jan	12-Jan	13-Jan	14-Jan
Week 3	15-Jan	16-Jan	17-Jan	18-Jan	19-Jan	20-Jan	21-Jan
Week 4	22-Jan	23-Jan	24-Jan	25-Jan	26-Jan	27-Jan	28-Jan

If you have 56 members in the group then all prayer and fasting slots will be covered as long as each member commits to pray within a minimum of two watch periods each week and chooses to fast at least once in four weeks. Our experience at City Gates Church is that the majority of members commit to more than two prayer slots per week.

ROLE OF THE OVERSEER

Outlined below is what we posted to the group when we needed to get some more overseers on board.

- The overseers normally post the list of people who will be praying at the start of the watch for example at 12 midnight. They also post the list of prayer points as agreed in the overseers group.
- Following that, the overseers welcome the warriors when they join the tower; this would be when the warriors post *praying now*.
- At the end of the watch, for example at 3am, the overseer on watch hands over to the next overseer.
- Also if an overseer notices that someone listed hasn't been joining the watch regularly, then they check that everything is okay.

In order not to overburden the overseers, it is recommended that praying slots that they have committed to should be within the watches for which they have oversight.

At City Gates Church we have fourteen overseers in total including the two administrators. Although the watches in the more sociable hours for instance, 6am to 9am typically require just one overseer to cover the entire week, we have seven overseers sharing the 12 midnight to 3am watches each week to ensure that our approach remains sustainable.

Additionally we have an Overseers WhatsApp group which is used to facilitate coordination of key messages before they are circulated to the wider group.

ROLE OF THE ADMINISTRATOR

The administrators are also overseers who have the following additional responsibilities:

- Maintenance of the prayer and fasting rotas.
- Addition of new participants to the WhatsApp group; ensuring they are have clarity about the mission; understand the group guidelines and how it operates on a day-to-day basis.
- Management of key prayer updates and announcements.
- Liaison with the church leaders and other prayer teams in the church.

SAMPLE PRAYERS

Included in this section are some of the prayers we have posted and continue to post on the watchtower prayer forum:

1. Praying for our Local Community

Let us pray for Ilford and its neighbouring localities. Our local church is placed here for a reason. Let us pray for a **revival in Ilford**:

- Come **against prostitution** on our streets; that the Lord will reach the women through His word and His workers.
- Let us pray that His love touches them and fills the pain and lack of self worth or lack of guidance that may have led them to the streets.
- Let us pray for the Women on the Frontline (WOFL) team who are out there on weeknights: for their protection, for wisdom, discernment and for the opportunity to sow good seed.
- Come **against violence:** knife crimes, muggings, acid attacks.
- Come against **slavery, captivity and cruelty** in our communities.
- Pray for the **protection of the minds** of the youth

on these streets; come against radicalisation and false teaching.
- Pray for His Kingdom to come and for **His light to overcome the darkness**; for strongholds to be torn down.
- Pray for the **Gideons Bible Society** to gain access into our schools.

2. Praying for the Healing of our Land - United Kingdom

Let us **continue to** pray for the church as a body, our country and its leaders:

The Church[2]

- We want to confess our sins of compromise and silence, while the wicked have been so vocal.
- We confess lack of unity and embracing competition.
- We confess our idols and wrong priorities.
- We confess our lack of prayer and lack of Holy Spirit oil flowing in our lives and meetings.
- We confess our lack of readiness as the Bride of Christ.

---

[2] From the prayers circulated on http://propheticvision.org.uk ahead of the 08 Sep 2017 Day of Prayer for Britain, which we also joined with prayer and fasting. Used with permission.

Let us continue to bring the body of Christ and our land earnestly before the Lord in prayer; let us pray:

- For forgiveness on behalf of our Land.
- That judgement should not come upon our nation.
- For God to spare our nation and to save the people.
- For God to direct church leaders and the church as a whole on how to take our position as the salt and light.
- For the government/decision makers to be subject to His will.
- For restoration of our nation as we repent.

Let us pray in Jesus Name that **darkness is forced to hide** and that we take back what the enemy has stolen. Let your kingdom come Lord; heal our land!

3. Pushing back the darkness AND Protecting the next generation

"Jesus said, "Let the little children come to me, and do not hinder them, for the kingdom of heaven belongs to such as these."" *Matthew 19:14 NIV*

For the young generation and future generations, **let us pray**:

- Against the barrage of evil, sexualisation etc. targeting them from all forms of media, the

education system, legislation and every facet of the society.
- For protection of their minds, that they will **find their identity in Christ**, bringing an end to low self-esteem, lack of self-worth, depression and all forms of mental health issues.
- That the atmosphere will change - there will be **openness to the truth** and the word of God will be heard again across our nation.
- For the offspring of Christians: the evil in the wider society will not quash the seed of God's word from their hearts. They will receive Christ from a tender age and take a **bold stand for the Lord** like Daniel did.
- For an awakening in the Church so that
    - **Christian schools** will
        - know and understand God's will for children
        - not compromise on their stand for Christ
    - **New schools** based on the truth of God's word will **spring up** all across this nation.

4. Praying for the Persecuted

Almost on a daily basis we hear of believers being persecuted for standing up for the truth of the word of God. We need to lift up our fellow believers in prayer as instructed by the bible:

"Continue to remember those in prison as if you were together with them in prison, and those who are mistreated as if you yourselves were suffering." *Hebrews 13:3 NIV*

For the persecuted, **let us pray**

- The Lord will **arise on behalf of those** who are suffering persecution all across the UK at the moment. He will **uphold them and their families** and they would not despair.
- Christians will not be cowed by these incidents but rather like the Apostles we will be filled with the **Holy Spirit and boldness** to **evangelise openly** and to stand up for what we believe in.
- The body of Christ **will not be silenced** but will unite, speak with **one voice** and **stand together** to support the persecuted.
- Christian advocates with **brilliant minds and filled with the Holy Spirit** will arise to defend the persecuted.

5. Praying for Fruitful Evangelism

- Cover the **Street Evangelists** as they go out to Ilford every Friday and Saturday. For the good news they bring to be readily received.
- May the Lord level the mountains of 'false

beliefs', 'ideologies' and 'lies hidden in convincing arguments' that stand in their way.
- May the Holy Spirit be with them directing their path and giving them His words to say.
- Let their words fall on fertile soil because the Holy Spirit has already gone before them.

6. Praying for our local church

Hallelujah! Revival has begun in City Gates Church Let us:

- Thank God for what has begun in our midst.
- Come against every plan of the enemy to quench the fire of the Holy Ghost.
- Pray for **every leader and member** of our church:
   o for His forgiveness and cleansing from all unrighteousness
   o that we will be aligned with the will of God, respond to His voice and nothing of the flesh will prevail in our midst
   o for God to break our hearts with the things that break His heart
   o for His protection over us and our family members

7. Praising through to Victory

As we battle spiritually, let us continue to **worship and give exuberant praise** to our God. This is one of our strongest weapons of warfare.

"At the very moment they began to sing and give praise, the Lord caused the armies of Ammon, Moab, and Mount Seir to start fighting among themselves." *2 Chronicles 20:22 NLT*

As we lift up the name of Jesus, we believe that confusion will be thrown into the camp of the enemy. We have the victory in Jesus name!

SAMPLE GUIDELINES

Included in this section are some of the guidelines we have posted on the watchtower prayer forum in the past:

- Due to the size of this group, it is necessary to share some protocols; let us stay on point to pray together and hear from God together else we will lose focus.
- It is best to refrain from posting anything unrelated to our main prayer points to this group. Let us be mindful of others and not inundate them with irrelevant messages such that they miss the main updates, prayer points and prophecies.
- Videos take up a lot of memory; so if there is a relevant video to share, rather than post it, post the link to it.
- Please do not forward any chain chats/texts pictures, or viral news of any nature to the group.
- If you believe that an issue or situation from the news or a chain text falls under the main prayer points, please explain it in your own words and rephrase it as a prayer point.
- You may wish to include a link to the issue but

please do not forward chain chats / texts or the commentary other people have made on a news item.
- As we become more familiar it would still be expedient not to send general greetings e.g. Happy new day / weekend / new month etc. in order not to take up too much space on each other's phones.
- Also let us ensure that we do not speak negatively of any groups of people in our community, we are here to pray for the unsaved not to judge them.
- If you feel strongly about a topic, by all means encourage us to pray about it but do not post random and sensational messages that have been circulating for years and are mainly untrue. Too many of these circulating messages are hoaxes; if curious about them, do your due diligence by checking on Snopes[3].

---

[3] An online site for checking the validity of messages received. www.snopes.com

To get additional resources for

On the Watch

Go to www.theprayertower.com

- Get additional inspired prayer points
- Discover more tips on how to set up your own tower of prayer
- Connect with the community of Christians who are also praying for revival

Printed in Great
Britain
by Amazon